ar 2013

All about Spring

Weather in Spring

by Martha E. H. Rustad

Consulting Editor: Gail Saunders-Smith, PhD

Consultant: John D. Krenz, PhD
Department of Biological Sciences
Minnesota State University, Mankato

CAPSTONE PRESS
a capstone imprint

Pebble Plus is published by Capstone Press,
1710 Roe Crest Drive, North Mankato, Minnesota 56003.
www.capstonepub.com

Library of Congress Cataloging-in-Publication Data
Rustad, Martha E. H. (Martha Elizabeth Hillman), 1975-
Weather in spring / by Martha E.H. Rustad.
p. cm. — (Pebble plus. All about spring)
Includes bibliographical references and index.
ISBN 978-1-4296-8654-9 (library binding)
ISBN 978-1-4296-9364-6 (paperback)
ISBN 978-1-62065-289-3 (ebook PDF)
1. Spring—Juvenile literature. 2. Weather—Juvenile literature. I. Title.

QB637.5.R87 2013

551.6—dc23

2012000124

Summary: "Simple text and full-color photographs present weather in spring."

Editorial Credits
Shelly Lyons, editor; Bobbie Nuytten, designer; Svetlana Zhurkin, photo researcher; Kathy McColley,
     production specialist

Photo Credits
Capstone Press: Kim Brown, 6–7; Dreamstime: Elwynn, 1, Igor Kovalchuk, 4–5, Paradoks_blizanaca, cover;
iStockphoto: quavondo, 20–21; Shutterstock: bofotolux, 10–11, David Maska, 12–13, Laurent Dambies, 8–9,
Marish (green leaf), cover and throughout, mycola, 14–15, Todd Shoemake, 18–19, Vitaly Krivosheev, 16–17,
Zubada (leaf pattern), cover

Note to Parents and Teachers

The All about Spring series supports national science and social studies standards related to
changes during the seasons. This book describes and illustrates weather in spring. The images
support early readers in understanding the text. The repetition of words and phrases helps early
readers learn new words. This book also introduces early readers to subject-specific vocabulary
words, which are defined in the Glossary section. Early readers may need assistance to read
some words and to use the Table of Contents, Glossary, Read More, Internet Sites, and Index
sections of the book.

Printed in China.

032012   006677RRDF12

Table of Contents

It's Spring!

Spring is here.

The weather feels warmer.

The sun shines longer each day.

The Shining Sun

As Earth moves around the sun,

it spins on a tilted axis.

In spring, the sun shines

more directly on

the northern part of Earth.

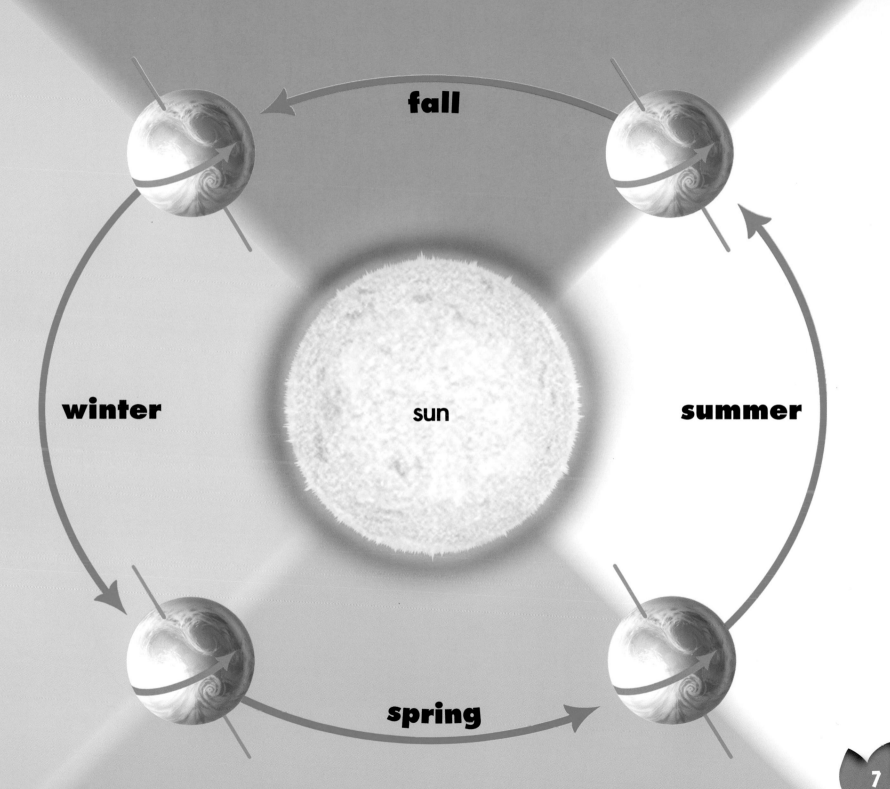

fall

winter

sun

summer

spring

The sun rises earlier each day.

It sets later every night.

Longer days bring
warmer weather.
Sunshine melts snow.

Water from melted snow runs
into creeks and rivers.
Sometimes waterways flood.

Spring Storms

Spring weather changes often.
Warm, sunny days follow
cool, rainy days.

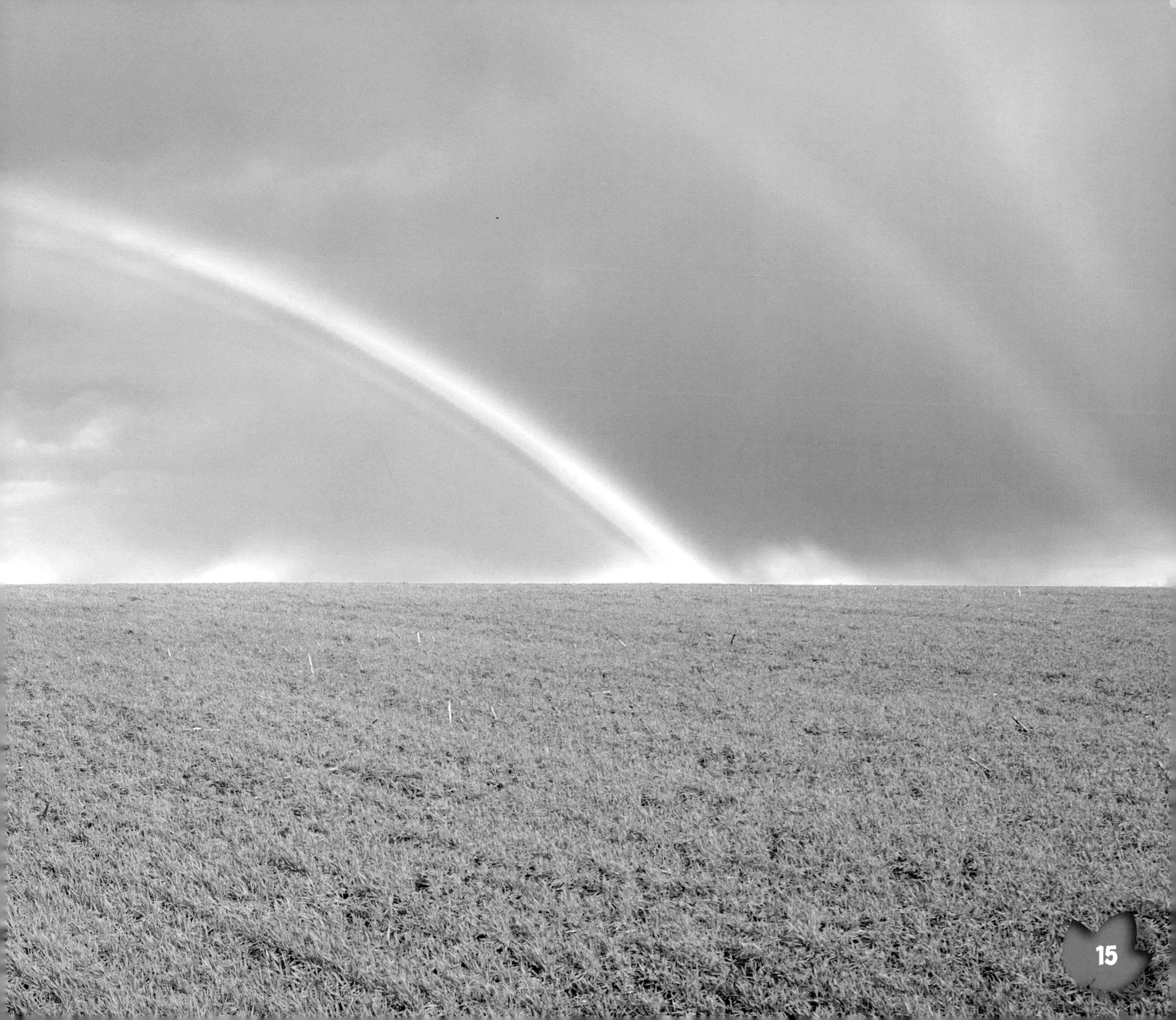

Storm clouds form.

Rain falls, lightning flashes,
and thunder rolls.

Small storms can become big storms. Tornadoes swirl.

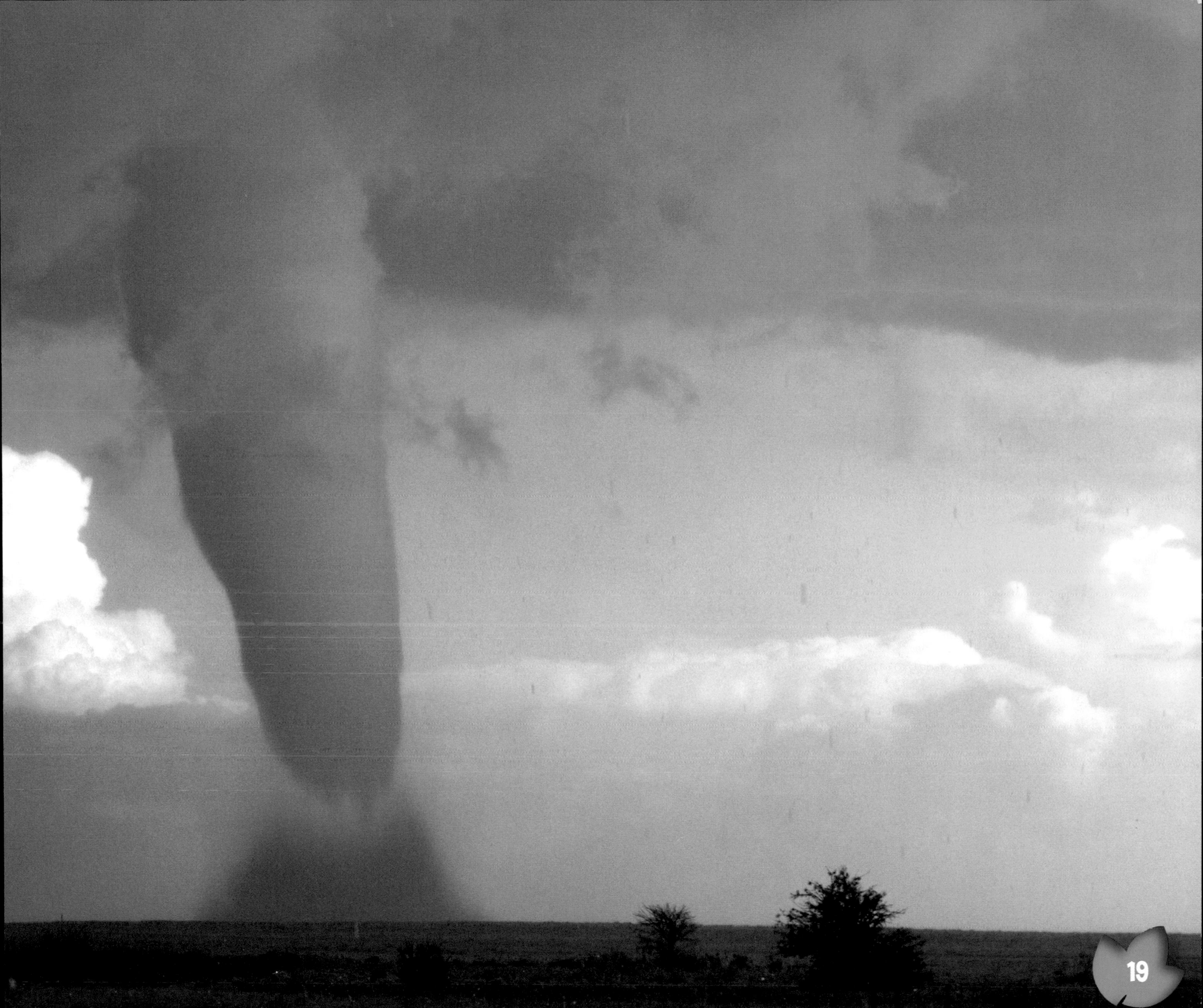

Your Spring

Spring can be

sunny, rainy, and stormy.

What weather does

spring bring to your home?

Glossary

axis—a real or imaginary line through an object's center, around which the object turns

direct—coming from a source without being blocked or reflected

flood—to overflow with water beyond the normal limits

lightning—a flash of electricity in the sky caused by electricity moving between clouds or between a cloud and the ground

tilt—leaning; not upright

tornado—a large, twisting funnel cloud with high winds; tornadoes that touch land can destroy anything in their paths

weather—the conditions outside at a certain time and place

Read More

Amoroso, Cynthia and Robert B. Noyed. *Spring*. Weather Watch. Mankato, Minn.: Child's World, 2010.

Latta, Sara L. *Why Is It Spring?* Why Do We Have Seasons? Berkeley Heights, N.J.: Enslow Publishers, Inc., 2012.

Smith, Siân. *Spring*. Seasons. Chicago: Heinemann Library, 2009.

Internet Sites

FactHound offers a safe, fun way to find Internet sites related to this book. All of the sites on FactHound have been researched by our staff.

Here's all you do:

Visit *www.facthound.com*

Type in this code: 9781429686549

Index

Word Count: 113
Grade: 1
Early-Intervention Level: 15